D0296198

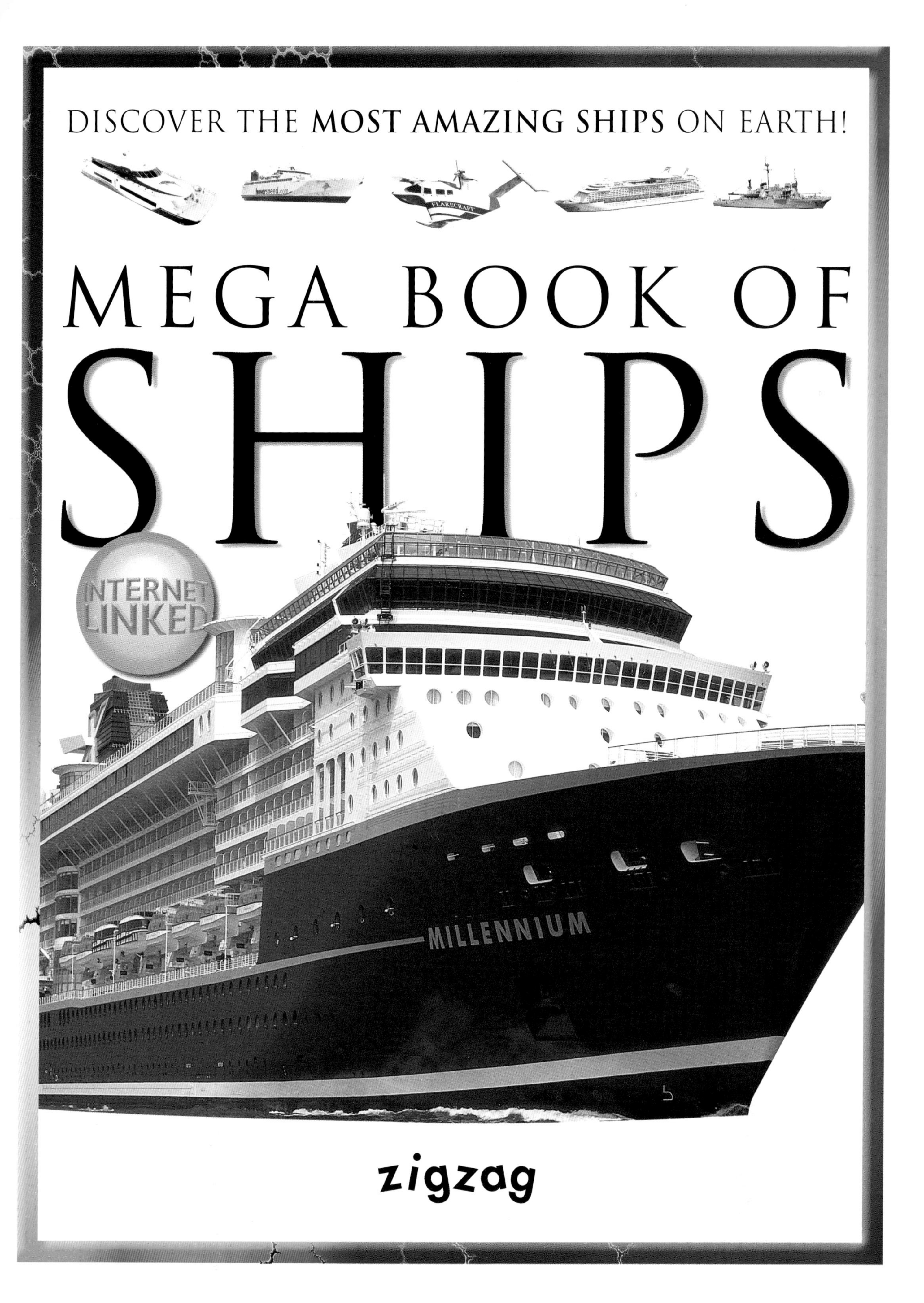
DISCOVER THE MOST AMAZING SHIPS ON EARTH!
MEGA BOOK OF
SHIPS
INTERNET LINKED
FLARECRAFT
MILLENNIUM
zigzag

INTERNET LINKS

http://www.transinst.org/seawords.htm
Find out the meanings of some old and new seafaring words, plus lots of other information about ships.

http://www.shipping.dft.gov.uk
For links to all kinds of nautical and maritime sites, where you'll find information on a whole range of shipping topics.

http://www.shipmodelers-assn.org
Find out more about some of the most famous ships in history.

http://www.encyclopedia-titanica.org
Find out about cruise ships, liners and vintage ships, plus personal accounts of trips onboard famous ships like the Constitution.

http://www.atomicengines.com
Read about the NS Savannah, the world's first nuclear-powered commercial ship.

http://www.ocean-liners.com
Interesting info about many of the big ships – both past and present!

http://www.photovault.com
Some great photographs of cargo ships, tankers – and lots of other ships, too!

http://www.factmonster.com
Enter 'steamships' to go to a great page about early steamships.

http://www.hover.globalinternet.co.uk
All the latest info on the hovercraft, including a hovercraft museum!

INTERNET SAFETY

Always follow these guidelines for a fun and safe journey through cyberspace:

1. Ask your parents for permission before you go online.
2. Spend time with your parents online, and show them your favourite sites.
3. Post your family's e-mail address, even if you have your own (only give your personal address to someone you trust).
4. Do not reply to e-mails if you feel they are strange or upsetting.
5. Do not use your real surname while you are online.
6. Never arrange to meet 'cyber friends' in person without your parents' permission.
7. Never give out your password.
8. Never give out your home address or telephone number.
9. Do not send scanned pictures of yourself unless your parents approve.
10. Leave a website straight away if you find something that is offensive or upsetting. Talk to your parents about it.

an imprint of Chrysalis Children's Books
64 Brewery Road, London N7 9NT

Author: Lynne Gibbs
Editorial Director: Honor Head
Art Director: Sophie Wilkins
Senior Editor: Rasha Elsaeed
Designer: Scott Gibson
Picture Researcher: Aline Morely

Every effort has been made to ensure none of the recommended websites in this book is linked to inappropriate material. However, due to the ever-changing nature of the Internet, the publishers regret they cannot take responsibility for future content of these websites. Therefore, it is strongly advised that children and parents consider the safety guidelines above.

British Library Cataloguing in Publication Data for this book is available from the British Library.

ISBN 1 903954 99 1

Printed and bound in Taiwan

CONTENTS

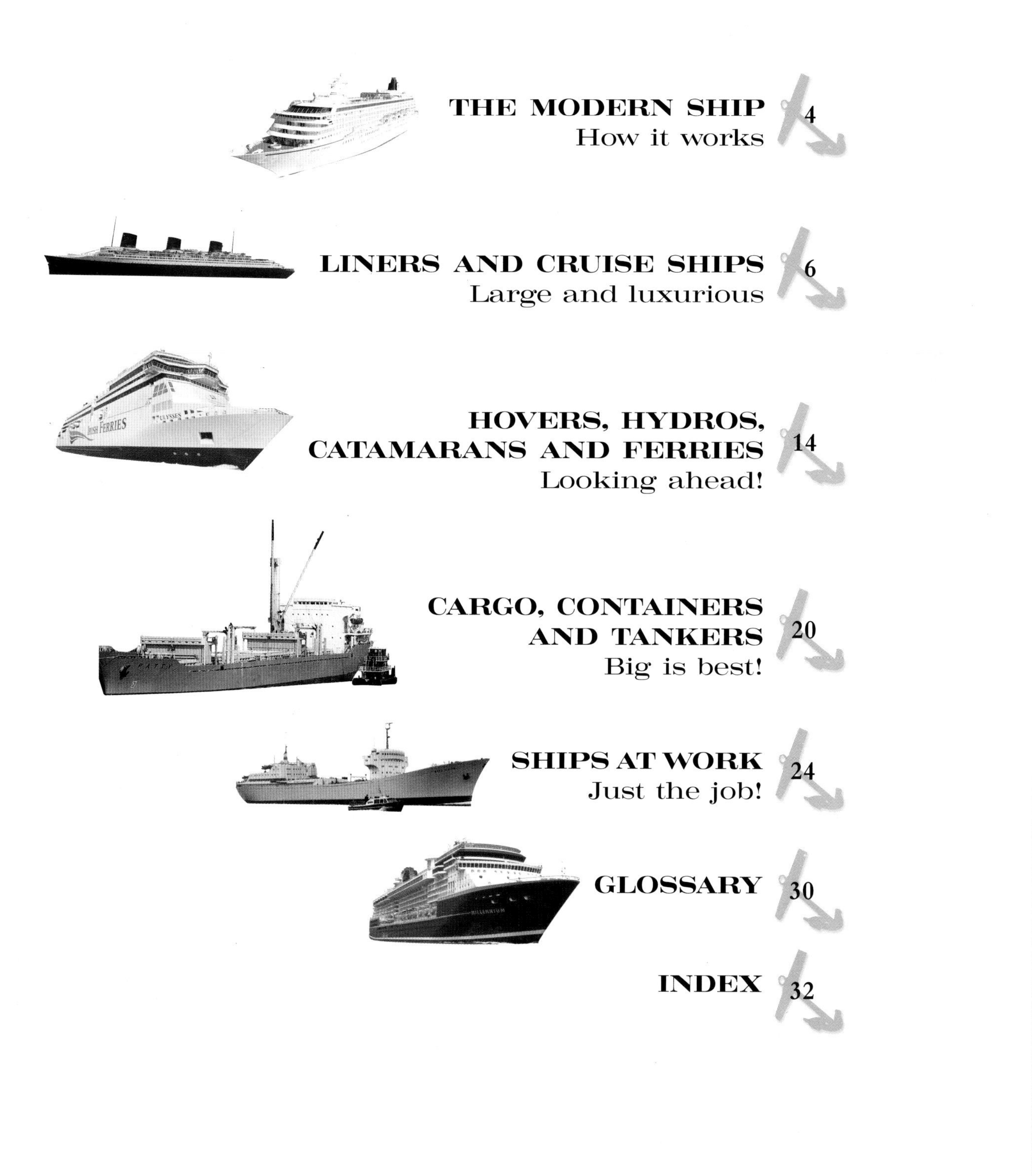

THE MODERN SHIP

MEGA FACT
In 1794 the Earl of Stanhope built a steam-powered vessel named the Kent. This was an experimental ship, which though not successful, showed designers how to develop others that were.

Since the wooden trading boats of the Ancient Egyptians, ships have been the main mode of travel across rivers and seas. The Phoenicians developed the galley, powered by oar and sail, the Ancient Greeks and Romans used their ships to trade around the Mediterranean, the Vikings explored the north Atlantic in longboats and the Chinese carried tonnes of cargo in their ships' hulls. From the early steamships to the latest liners, ships have become bigger, faster and more reliable than ever before. Over the following pages, you will discover how some of the greatest modern ships have changed the history of sea-going vessels.

FROM SAIL TO STEAM

During the reign of Queen Victoria, Britain was one of the world's leading industrial nations. As an island, most of her wealth depended on her merchant ships, which carried people and goods around her huge empire. British ships had to be among the best in the world, and using steam for propelling ships through the water was a great advantage.

How a diesel engine works

Diesel engines are used to power anything from small machinery to huge ships. All diesel engines work on the same principle, the biggest difference being their size, as you can see by the man standing beside this ship's huge engine! A diesel engine, which has no spark plug, takes in air, compresses it and then injects fuel directly into the compressed air. The heat of the compressed air lights the fuel spontaneously.

- Fuel oil
- Lubricating oil
- Exhaust gas
- Jacket water
- Sea/fresh water
- Starting air
- Scavenge air

SYMPHONY

MEGA BRIGHT

Thomas Alva Edison (1847–1931) invented the forerunner of the gramophone, the first electric filament bulb, the radio tube and a method of telegraphic messaging between moving ships and trains. Yet, he had only three months' official schooling in his life!

EVERYTHING YOU NEED!

With passenger capacities ranging from 400 to 3,000 people, standard cruise ships are categorised by their size, number of cabins, public room characteristics and onboard amenities. Onboard characteristics vary from ship to ship. Designed to be self-contained floating resorts, cruise ships need to be capable of spending several days or more at sea.

MEGA FACT

Dug out of the sandy desert, the Suez Canal allows ships to travel from the Mediterranean to the Red Sea instead of going all the way around Africa.

LINERS AND CRUISE SHIPS

In the early 20th century, huge liners carried hundreds of people across vast oceans. While third class (steerage) passengers lived in basic, overcrowded conditions, first class ticket holders travelled in luxury. By the mid 1960s, as air travel became cheaper and faster, ocean liners were soon replaced by cruise liners. Today, with every conceivable facility onboard, passengers often only go ashore to see the sights as the ship makes short stops in different countries.

MEGA FACT

The Chinese were the first people to use the compass in the 4th century BC, which consisted of a magnetised iron needle floating in a bowl of water.

MEGA FACT

Most Victorian steamships carried sails in case of engine failure. These were also used to get extra power if there were favourable winds.

GONE TO GROUND

The Queen Elizabeth liner was to have served out her days as a university in Hong Kong. But she was set on fire and sank in the harbour.

First ship builders

The ancient Egyptians were the first to build 'real ships'. They used wooden planks that were curved at both ends. The vessels, used to sail up and down the Nile and across the sea to trade with other countries, often had huge masts held in place by ropes. Square sails helped the winds push the ships along, while men at the stern used paddles to steer the ship through the water.

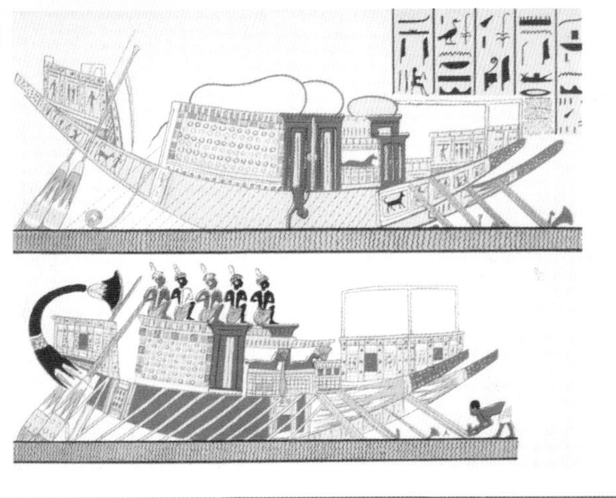

LUXURY LINER

The Normandie was designed to be the biggest, fastest and most beautiful liner in the world. Launched on 29 October 1932, she was the first ship to exceed 300m in length. The huge, 80,000-tonne French liner had 12 decks and could carry 1,975 passengers, plus around 1,345 crew. Each of her four powerful turbo-electric engines were connected to a separate propeller shaft, giving a total of 160,000hp. With a top speed of 32.2 knots, the grand liner used 5,000 tonnes of oil per transatlantic crossing.

MEGA FACT

During the 1950s, the Australian government encouraged people to settle in their country. Thousands of people used passenger liners to make their journey, as they offered cheap fares.

SUPER CRUISER

Launched in 1988, the Grand Princess is one of the largest passenger ships in the world. Taller than the Statue of Liberty and longer than three football fields, the super liner has the capacity for 2,600 passengers.

NORMANDIE

Built to provide 1,975 passengers with the ultimate in high-speed luxury, the Normandie was serviced by a crew of over 300 and nearly 1,000 domestic staff. During World War II, the US Army seized the Normandie and stripped out her luxurious trappings and expensive furnishings. Converted into a troopship, Normandie was then renamed USS Lafayette. The grand public rooms were intended to accommodate thousands of American and foreign GIs, but during the conversion work, a fire broke out aboard and smothered the ship in suffocating smoke.

MEGA STAR

Built in 1906, the Mauritania was the most famous Atlantic-crossing ship. Accommodating 560 first-class passengers, she had a crew of 812. The ship won the 'Blue Riband of the Atlantic' from the Kaiser Wilhelm II and held it for 22 years.

Cleveland

The Hamburg-Amerika Line's Cleveland was one of the first cargo liners to carry passengers and refrigerated cargo. The 17,000-tonne ship was built with accommodation for 250 first-class passengers, 392 second class, 494 third class and 2,064 emigrants. The emigrants who travelled in the crowded steerage space of most ships were kept out of view of those who paid higher fares. The Cleveland had a good standard of safety, but some older ships, no longer fit for use, were bought cheaply and patched up for carrying the thousands of emigrants that needed to travel. Not surprisingly, many died during the long, gruelling journey.

Blue Riband Award

During the 19th and early 20th centuries, the passenger shipping lines of Europe and America were competing to provide the fastest, most luxurious passenger service across the North Atlantic. Competition was fierce for the coveted 'Blue Riband of the Atlantic', awarded to the liner making the fastest crossing. The Mauritania held the Riband from 1907 until 1929, and had a top speed of 50 km/h.

QUEEN ELIZABETH 2

The QE2 was launched in 1970 to replace the Queen Mary and the Queen Elizabeth. Although smaller than her two predecessors, she is still a huge ship at 65,000 tonnes gross. With 12 passenger decks, 750 staterooms and the capacity to carry up to 1,892 passengers, the QE2 was the first liner built to combine the tasks of a transatlantic passenger liner and a luxury holiday cruise ship. During the Falkland Islands operations of 1982, the Ministry of Defence used her as a fast troopship to carry 3,000 soldiers 12,875km non-stop to the fighting front. At a cruising speed of 28.5 knots, the QE2 made this journey faster than any other ship at the time.

MEGA FACT

The Panama Canal links the Pacific and the Atlantic Oceans so that ships do not have to go all the way around South America.

MEGA FACT
Englishman John Wilkinson built the first iron boat, named 'The Trial' in 1787.

UNITED STATES

Costing a staggering US$74 million to build in 1952, the United States was the largest and fastest liner ever built. Following huge publicity, the ship's inaugural voyage was sold out well in advance. Living up to her owners' expectations, the United States steamed the 2,942 nautical miles from Ambrose Lightship to Bishop Rock in 3 days, 10 hours and 40 minutes, at an average speed of 35.59 knots. She made the crossing back in 3 days, 12 hours and 12 minutes at an average speed of 34.51 knots – winning the 'Blue Riband' from the Queen Mary.

TITANIC

White Star Line's ship Titanic sailed on her fateful first voyage to New York from Queenstown, Ireland, on 11 April 1912. Onboard were 1,318 passengers and a crew of 885. Four days later, the ship struck an iceberg off the Newfoundland coast, ripping a hole in the ship's starboard side, below the waterline. In under three hours, the Titanic broke in half and sank. At that time, regulations stated that the number of lifeboats carried on a ship was dependent upon the tonnage of the vessel and not the number of passengers. This meant the Titanic had only enough lifeboats for half the people onboard, leaving 916 passengers and 673 of the crew to die in the freezing water.

Parsons' Turbine Engines

All steam engines, including turbines, are powered by high-pressure steam being allowed to expand. Before Charles Parsons' invention, patented in 1884, turbine designs had been inefficient. Parsons realised that this was because the steam was expanded in a single step. He believed that if steam was allowed to expand gradually, then higher efficiencies could be reached. Parsons' prototype had fifteen stages of expansion. The steam expanded through successive rings of moving blades on a shaft and fixed blades in a casing, producing purely rotary movement.

LUSITANIA

The Lusitania and her sister Mauritania were the first liners to use the Parsons' steam turbine. Launched on 7 June 1906, the Lusitania was the largest vessel afloat at the time. Marking her a pioneer in maritime history, the ship's quadruple-screw propulsion unit was driven by direct-drive steam turbines that could drive the Lusitania at 25 knots. During World War I, the ship set off on its last voyage, sailing from New York, USA, on 1 May 1941. By 7 May, with 1,959 passengers onboard, the ship had entered enemy waters. A torpedo fired by an enemy submarine hit the ship and the Lusitania sank, killing 1,198 people.

MEGA FACT

After the tragic sinking of the Titanic, new regulations required ships to carry sufficient lifeboats to carry everyone onboard. The wreck of the Titanic was discovered on 1 September 1985.

QUEEN MARY

The Queen Mary could travel at a speed of over 30 knots. The liner made its maiden voyage on 27 May 1936, on the Southampton-Cherbourg-New York route. In the first year of service, the ship had carried 56,895 passengers. After making her last commercial voyage from Southampton on 30 August 1939, the Queen Mary was converted into a World War II troopship. During its war service, the ship travelled over 600,000 miles and carried nearly 800,000 people. On 27 September 1946 the Queen Mary was handed back to Cunard, the shipping cruise line. After making her last transatlantic crossing on 16 September 1967, the liner was sold to the town of Long Beach, USA, where she now stands as a museum, hotel and conference centre.

MEGA FACT

The Sirius, a small 700-tonne paddler, was the first steam-powered ship to cross the Atlantic.

SS Great Western

The Great Western Steamship Company was founded in 1836 as a sea extension of the Great Western Railway, to build a steamship to cross the Atlantic, from Bristol, England. Designed by Isambard Kingdom Brunel, the Great Western was launched in 1837. A wooden auxiliary paddle steamer, she was remarkable for her great strength. In 1838 the ship crossed from Bristol to New York in around 151 days. The SS Great Western was the first steamship constructed for transatlantic service and carried 148 passengers.

MEGA POWER

Ships that need to travel fast like ferries, hovercrafts and warships usually have gas turbine engines. Turbines allow a ship to go faster because of their small size and light weight. These types of engines can be up to 80 per cent lighter and 60 per cent smaller than diesel engines of the same power.

Ships and other structures

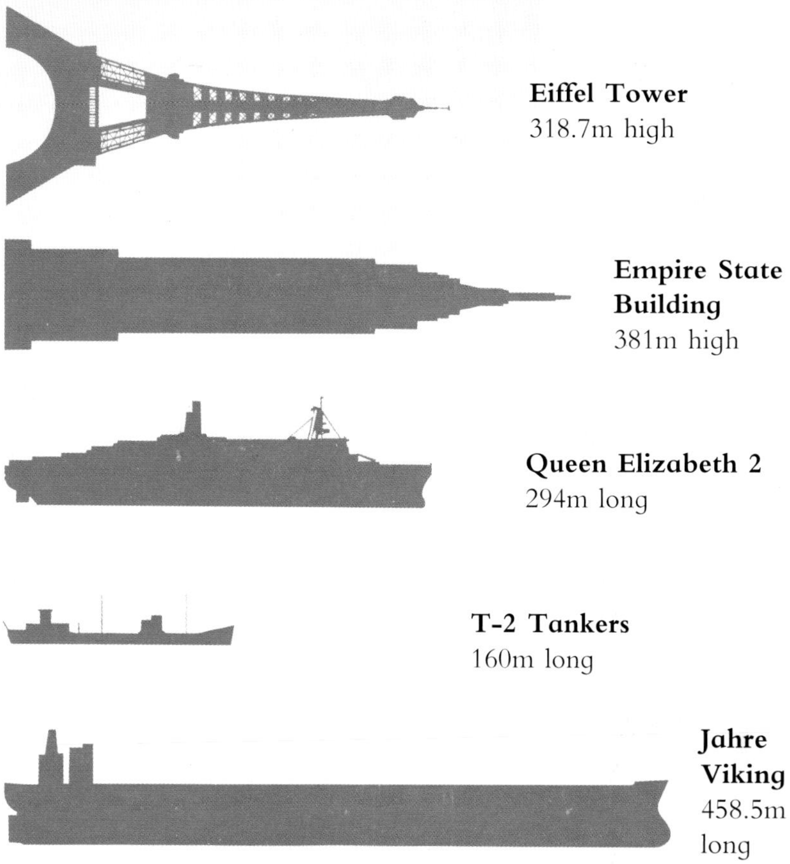

Eiffel Tower
318.7m high

Empire State Building
381m high

Queen Elizabeth 2
294m long

T-2 Tankers
160m long

Jahre Viking
458.5m long

EXPLORER OF THE SEAS

This luxury cruise liner, with its own diesel-electric power station, was launched on 28 October 2000. The ship has a total length of 311.1m, a breadth of 38.6m and a height from the keel to the funnel top of 72.3m. Explorer of the Seas has a passenger capacity of 3,840 and a crew capacity of 1,180 – a total of 5,020 people! Among the many facilities onboard is a theatre seating up to 1,350 people, an ice-skating rink, 'street' fair, four pools, a children's adventure beach, rock-climbing wall, hospital and wedding chapel!

HOVERS, HYDROS, CATAMARANS AND FERRIES

Using the latest technology, ship builders and designers are creating new types of hovercraft, hydrofoils, catamarans and ferries. These powerful, futuristic sea vessels are able to travel extremely fast over long distances and can carry everything from cargo loads to vehicles and passengers. Navies all over the world are also working on designs for hovercrafts, hydrofoils and catamarans that can be used during peacetime as well as wartime.

MEGA FACT
The hovercraft's skirt was invented by CH Latimer-Needham.

ULYSSES
Ferries are becoming bigger, faster and more luxurious than ever before. Towering over other vessels at a height of 51m from keel to mast, Ulysses has almost 5km of parking space – enough room for 1,342 cars or 240 articulated trucks per sailing.

MEGA LIFT
When a hydrofoil gathers speed, the foils under its bow lift the vessel out of the water. Because the hydrofoil is almost out of the water, it is able to travel very fast.

How a hovercraft works

Although hovercraft are large enough to carry cars, the vehicles must be carefully arranged on the car deck so as to distribute their weight evenly. Flying about three metres above the water, powerful engines turn huge fans that push air down and underneath the hovercraft. The pressure of this air is slightly higher than the surrounding air so the hovercraft rises up. The skirt around the craft traps the air and keeps the pressure under the craft higher than it is outside. The flexible skirt acts like a shock absorber so the craft can move smoothly. The engines also turn propellers that push the hovercraft forward and steer it.

FERRY BIG

Ulysses, a roll-on/roll-off cargo- and passenger-carrying ship, is the largest car ferry in the world. After almost a year in construction, the total cost of the vessel when launched on 1 September 2000 was £100 million! The futuristic ferry, standing 12 decks high, has a gross tonnage of 50,938 tonnes.

MEGA FACT

In Jume 1990, a catamaran called the Hoverspeed Great Britain won the Hales Blue Riband award for the fastest crossing of the Atlantic Ocean. The vessel took three days, seven hours and 54 minutes!

ULYSSES

Named after James Joyce's novel of the same name, Ulysses has the capacity to carry 1,875 passengers and 125 crew. Facilities include restaurants, shopping mall, cinema, casino, first-aid centre and a helicopter-landing space. The ferry can cross the Irish Sea with two return trips between Dublin Port and Holyhead each day. This means that in one day, she has the capacity to transport 5,368 cars or 960 articulated trucks!

MEGA FACT
On just one trip from Dover to Calais, the Pride of Calais superferry can carry up to 2,300 passengers and 650 cars.

THE SR-N1 HOVERCRAFT

The hovercraft was the creation of Sir Christopher Cockrell, who first experimented with air films under model boats to give a kind of lubricated surface. Then in 1954 he tried using fixed side walls with water curtains and hinged end doors with air pumped into the centre. This led him to consider using air curtains. He made a model out of two empty coffee tins and a small, industrial fan dryer – and it worked! Cockrell applied for his first patent in 1955 and his first working vessel was called the Saunders Roe-Nautical One (SR-N1).

Travelling light

Catamarans have two narrow hulls running along their length, joined by the main part of the ship. This design spreads the weight of the ship over a large area. Because the hulls are narrow, they displace less water than an ordinary ship with the same capacity. This reduces the drag of the water, enabling catamarans to travel at high speeds.

MEGA FACT

Arab seamen in the Red Sea were the first to use triangular sails. A triangular sail was more efficient than a square sail, which only works well if the wind is behind a ship.

FLYING DOLPHIN 2000

Flying Dolphin 2000 connects Piraeus with the Greek islands Poros, Hydra, Spetses and Port-Heli. The all-passenger vessel was designed to combine luxurious accommodation with high-speed performance. Because there are no trailers and cars to load, she only needs a crew of nine. With an overall length of 47.6m, the vessel is powered by four MTU 16-valve, four-stroke 4000 M70 engines, positioned two in each hull. The ferry can achieve a top speed of around 45 knots and is fitted with four mini evacuation slides and 12 life rafts, each holding up to 50 people.

MEGA FACT

Captain James Cook was the first European to sail Australia.

THE PRIDE OF HULL

Among the largest ferries in the world, the Pride of Hull and her sister ship the Pride of Rotterdam were built to work between the ports of Hull and Rotterdam. The construction of the ferries was carried out in Venice. The enormous ferries, which each took less than 14 months to build, have an overall length of 215.1m. Based over 12 decks, the entertainment facilities include cyber cafes, shops, casinos, cinemas, restaurants and fully-equipped business centres. Both vessels are powered by four Wartsila NSD 9L46C engines, which deliver a total output of 37,800kW at 500rpm, and have 546 cabins and 1,376 beds.

VILLUM CLAUSEN

Constructed in Australia, the Villum Clausen was the first gas turbine-powered vehicle ferry to be built in the Southern Hemisphere. The vessel entered service in April 2000. During the delivery voyage, Villum Clausen established a new record for the longest distance travelled by a ship in 24 hours. On 16 and 17 February 2000, the ferry covered 1,063 nautical miles between Sumatra and Cochin, achieving a maximum speed of 47.7 knots. The maximum vehicle payload of 380 tonnes would typically comprise 186 cars or a combination of 144 cars, 10 coaches or trucks weighing up to 20 tonnes and 15 motorcycles.

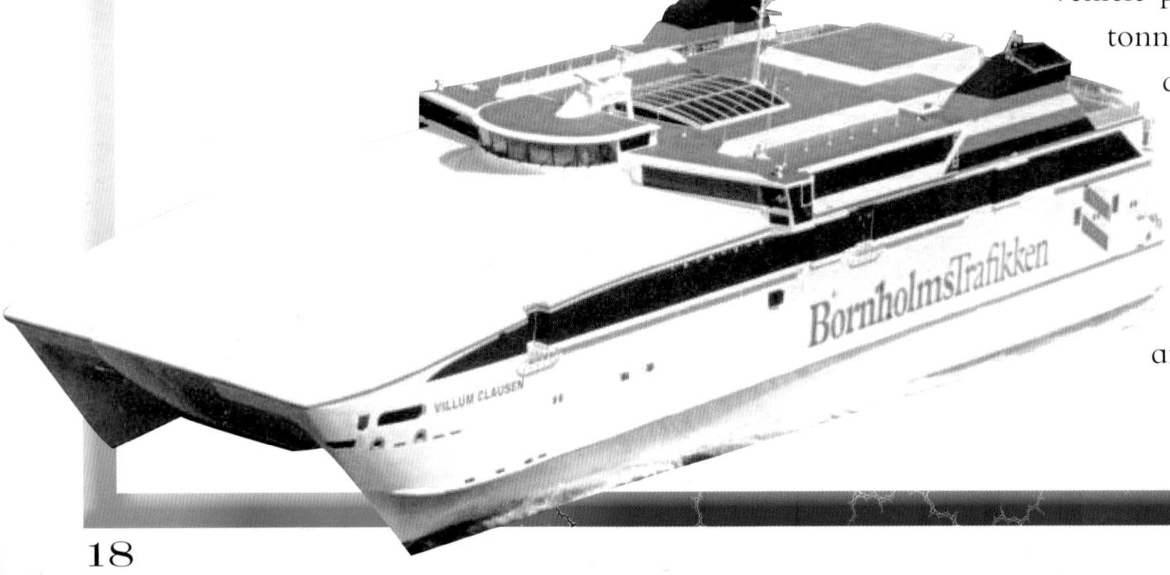

First hydrofoil

Designed and built by Italian engineer Enrico Forlanini, the first hydrofoil used a ladder system of foils and a 60hp engine driving two counter-rotating air props. During testing in 1906, Forlanini's craft, which was quite basic compared to the hydrofoils of today, reached a top speed of 42.5 mph. In 1911, Alaxander Graham Bell began testing the HD-1, a hydrofoil with short airfoils plus hydrofoils, to help in lift. The craft reached 50 m/ph using an air propeller. Intending this technology to be used as an aid to sailing, Graham Bell envisioned large passenger hydrofoils sailing across the Atlantic without the need for an engine.

SUPERSEACAT

The first of these 100 metres-long, mono-hull fast ferries was launched in 1977. Built in Italy, the SuperSeaCat's hull and superstructure are fabricated from aluminium alloys instead of high-tensile steel. With a capacity for 782 passengers, 26 crew and 175 cars, the ferry has a maximum continuous speed of 40 knots at full load. The SuperSeaCat has two main engine rooms, which can operate independently and is powered by four Ruston 20RK270 diesel engines. Each main engine drives a KaMeWa S112 waterjet unit via a Renk PLS 50z-reduction gearbox. Electrical power is provided from three 340kW generators.

MEGA WEIRD

Catamarans were developed in the Pacific islands thousands of years ago. They have only been used in the rest of the world during the last 35 years.

MEGA FACT

A type of hydrofoil called a stabiliser is used on ocean-crossing passenger ships to minimise wave action on the vessel.

CARGO, CONTAINERS AND TANKERS

The world's largest ships are cargo carriers, and the largest ships of all are oil tankers. These modern ships are expensive to build, so they spend as little time as possible idling in port. However, because they use the latest computerised control and navigation systems, these vessels are able to sail with only a handful of crew.

MEGA FACT
The huge metal crates loaded onto container ships come in two standard sizes, one container exactly twice the size of the other.

FACTORY FISHING SHIPS

At one time, fishermen out in their ships had to return to land as quickly as possible, where they could clean and freeze their catch of fish. This meant that the fishermen were limited to travelling within a certain area, as they had to return while their catch was fresh. Today, large 'factory' fishing ships are able to process the fish while still at sea. This ensures that the fish remains perfectly 'fresh'.

Tugs

Ocean-going ships are so big that they are difficult to steer in enclosed waters and often have trouble sailing in and out of port. This is where tugs come in. Tugs are stubby little boats that handle so well, they can work in even the tightest spaces – alongside piers, closed-off sections of canals, rivers and locks. Tucked into a tug's hull is an incredibly powerful engine that drives a huge propeller. This provides the power to tow cargo ships and oil tankers well over a hundred times as heavy as the tug.

SELF-CONTAINED!

To make loading quicker, most freight goes onboard in large, pre-packaged metal containers. With their huge hulls and decks, many modern container ships have enough room for over 6,000 containers.

MEGA FACT

Ships that carry only one kind of cargo are called 'bulk carriers'.

MEGA FAR

A big oil tanker ships about 132 million litres of petrol – enough to drive a car 47,000 times around the earth.

MEGA FAR
Some builders of large Japanese tankers issue their crew with bicycles to travel around the huge ships.

READY FOR THE RETAILERS

As the huge fishing nets are wound in, the fish are removed and conveyed to a processing deck onboard the ship. Here the fish are scaled, cleaned and filleted. They are then packed into boxes and frozen in the cold store in the hold, ready for delivery to outlets on land.

Torrey Canyon

Built in North America in 1959 the Torrey Canyon was the first of the big supertankers, with a cargo capacity of 60,000 tonnes. She was later expanded to twice that capacity in Japan, giving 63,000 tonnes for the ship and 120,000 for the cargo. On 18 March 1967 the oil tanker, travelling at a speed of 17 knots, struck Pollard's Rock in the Seven Stones reef between the Scilly Isles and Land's End, England, tearing open six tanks. Over the next few weeks, all the oil escaped. The oil spread along the shores of the south coast of England and the Normandy coast of France and killed most of the marine life in the region. Because no set plans had been made for a disaster of this type and size, several different emergency measures were attempted. But these only made matters worse. Chemical dispersants sprayed onto the oil slicks proved to be more lethal than the original oil.

Oil spills

Oil floats on salt water (the ocean) and usually floats on fresh water (rivers and lakes). Oil spreads rapidly across the water surface to form a thin layer called an 'oil slick'. As the spreading continues, the layer becomes thinner, finally becoming a rainbow-coloured 'sheen'. To stop oil spreading further, attempts may be made to set fire to the oil with rockets from aircraft. Detergent can also be sprayed on the oil to prevent it coming ashore and ruining beaches. More recent methods of dealing with such spillage include drawing a boom around the oil to contain it and sinking the oil by adding ash deposits from furnaces. Oil tankers like the Magdala move huge cargoes of crude oil all around the world. Oil spillage in open sea therefore causes wide-spread global damage. One of the largest oil spills was caused by the Exxon Valdez. On 24 March 1989, the medium-sized oil tanker ran aground in Prince William Sound in the Gulf of Alaska, USA, spilling over 41 million litres of oil. The resulting slick covered more than 1,000 miles of the Alaska coastline and cost billions of pounds in environmental damages.

SALVAGE VESSELS

Salvage vessels are used for the underwater recovery of a ship and her contents or to assist vessels that are sinking or disabled at sea. Salvage tugs help search for wreckage and survivors when ships have sunk or aircraft have gone down over the sea. The most common causes of casualty are machinery breakdown at sea, hull damage and cargo shifting from storms. Recovery usually requires taking the ship under tow and bringing it into port. Many salvage vessels in service today carry a magnetic detector to locate metal debris.

MEGA USEFUL

The world uses nearly three billion gallons of oil every day. We use oil to:

- *Make medicines, ink, fertilisers, pesticides, paints and varnishes.*
- *Fuel our cars, trucks and buses.*
- *Heat our homes.*
- *Lubricate machinery such as bicycles and printing presses.*
- *Make asphalt to pave roads.*
- *Make plastics toys, portable radios and CD players.*
- *Electricity.*

SHIPS AT WORK

From the invention of the sailing ship, it took thousands of years to build a simple steamship. Then, within a relatively short period of time, ships using nuclear and gas turbine engines and super-conducting electromagnetic thrusters appeared. Today, there are ships that can 'fly' and the technology to produce catamarans that carry cargo! In the future, ships may be able to use energy from the Sun. These will burn hydrogen in special engines and the only exhaust would be water.

MEGA FACT
Inboard diesel engines are used to power all kinds of sea vessels, from yachts and fishing boats to tugs and tankers. These engines are strong, low on maintenance costs and use relatively little fuel.

THUMBS DOWN!
Although development of nuclear merchant ships began in the 1950s, it has not been commercially successful. This is due to public resistance to the general use of nuclear fuel as well as the reluctance of commercial ports to handle nuclear-powered ships like the Otto Hahn, fearing the possibility of radioactive leakage.

Steaming ahead

In 1790, John Fitch ran the first steamship service up the Delaware river in the USA. Around that time in America, the easiest way to travel was by river, so many new paddle steamers were built. Flowing from Canada and North America to the Gulf of Mexico, the Mississippi river is famous for its colourful steamboats. Powered by a large paddle wheel at the stern, these vessels first steamed out of New Orleans in 1812. Today, tourists can still travel on the world's largest riverboat, the 116-m long Mississippi Queen.

NUCLEAR-POWERED COMMERCIAL SHIPS

Although the initial installation is expensive, and the shielding that must enclose a ship's reactor is large and heavy, a nuclear-powered vessel has the advantage of being able to operate for up to two years without refuelling. With the rising cost of conventional, carbon-based fuel, this could be an attractive alternative for ship builders.

MEGA FACT

Whatever their cargo, the basic tanker design is the same. Cargo is carried in insulated tanks, or compartments, within the main tank that forms the largest part of the hull.

OTTO HAHN

Commissioned in 1962, the United States built the nuclear-powered ship NS Savannah. Although the vessel was a technical success, it was not economically viable and was decommissioned eight years later. The German-built Otto Hahn cargo ship and research facility sailed some 650,000 nautical miles on 126 voyages in 10 years without any technical problems. This ship also proved too expensive to operate and was later converted to diesel.

CABLE INNOVATOR CABLE LAYER

The Cable Innovator is the world's largest vessel of its kind, specifically designed for fibre-optic cable laying. Built by Kvaerner Masa of Finland, the vessel can operate in extreme weather and is equipped to deploy a remotely operated vehicle (ROV). The Cable Innovator has a conventional set of cable working instrumentation and two computerised cable instrumentation systems. It is powered by five Wartsila Vasa diesel engines, which provide a total power of 12.8MW. The ship has no rudder, but there are two tunnel thrusters located at the stern.

STANISLAV YUDIN

This Ice class III A2 crane vessel flies under the Russian Flag. Built in 1985, the Stanislav Yudin was upgraded in 1993 and 1996. With a maximum transit speed of 12 knots, the ship has been employed for platform installations and removals, salvage and installation of large sub-sea structures and in-shore lifting. With an overall length of 183.2 metres, the Stanislav Yudin can accommodate 135 people. It has its own helicopter deck and is equipped with an active computerised lifting analysing system, also suitable for simulation of load conditions. The vessel is offered for installation work in the North Sea, West Africa, Mediterranean, Middle East and Gulf of Mexico.

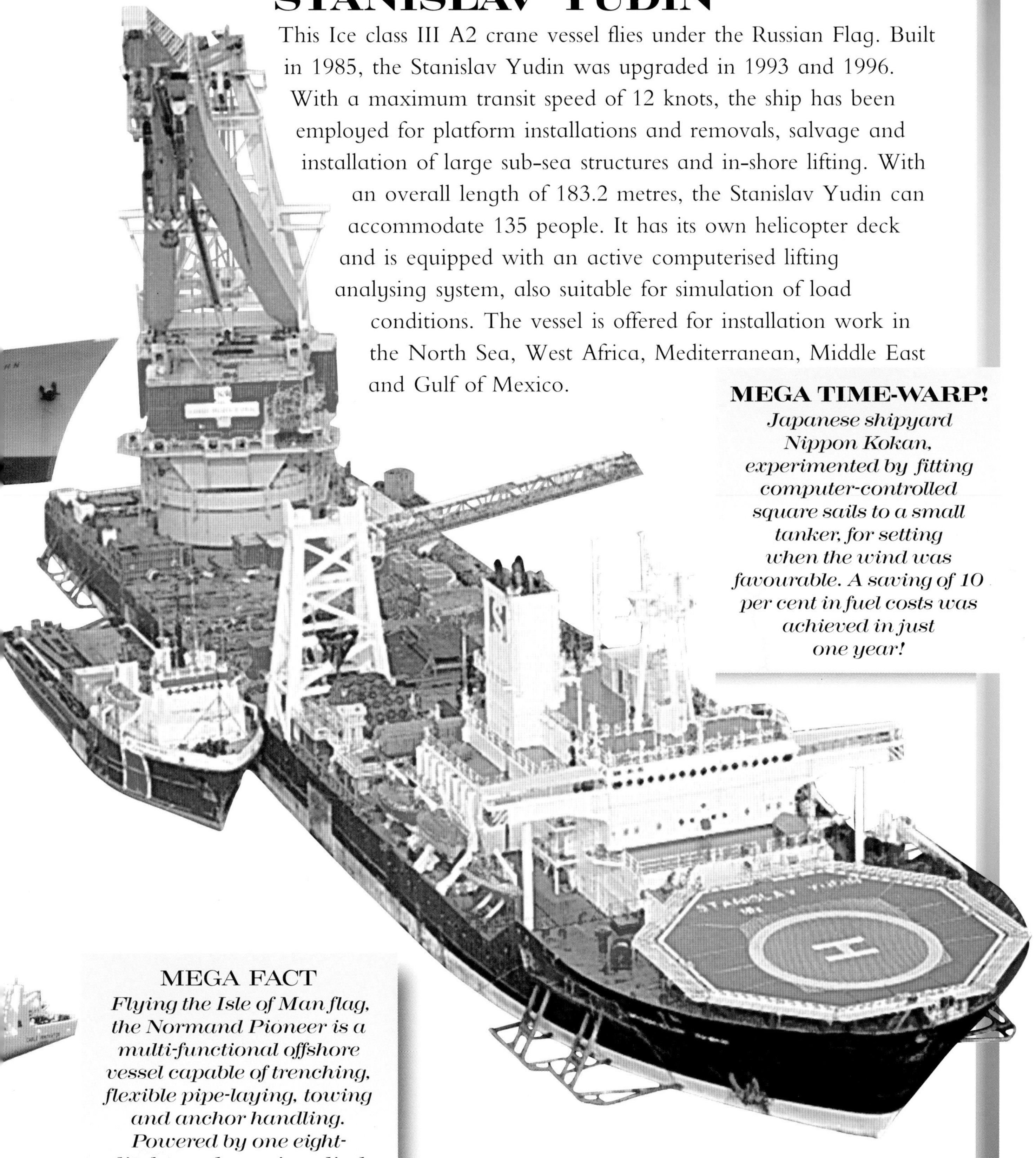

MEGA TIME-WARP!

Japanese shipyard Nippon Kokan, experimented by fitting computer-controlled square sails to a small tanker, for setting when the wind was favourable. A saving of 10 per cent in fuel costs was achieved in just one year!

MEGA FACT

Flying the Isle of Man flag, the Normand Pioneer is a multi-functional offshore vessel capable of trenching, flexible pipe-laying, towing and anchor handling. Powered by one eight-cylinder and one six-cylinder Wartsila SW38 engine, the Normand Pioneer has two tunnel thrusters and an Azimuthing thruster forward and two tunnel thrusters aft.

WIG CRAFT

The first serious WIG ('wing-in-ground' effect) boats were developed in the 1960s. The FlareCraft is one of a new kind of WIG craft that combines the speed of an aeroplane with the characteristics of a boat. A 225-hp engine provides power for 'flight' and propels the vessel to speeds in excess 160 km/h. But the FlareCraft cannot fly higher than 2m above the waves, which is why it is registered as a sea vessel. Other ship companies are developing similar WIG vessels, capable of carrying cargo and passengers.

JAHRE VIKING

The world's biggest tanker operating today is the Jahre Viking. Formerly known as Happy Giant and Seawise Giant, the already enormous vessel was converted in 1980 from another tanker by the insertion of an additional mid-ship section. This increased the overall length of the ship to 458.5 metres. Now measuring 260,851 gross register tonnes, Jahre Viking has a dead-weight tonnage (cargo capacity) of 564,763 tonnes.

MEGA FACT

Most ships today are fitted with radar. This shows the captain if there is another ship nearby so the ship can turn away to avoid a collision.

Ice-breaking power

Nuclear propulsion of ships was born out of the research into the atomic bombs that were dropped on Japan at the end of World War II. Although the use of nuclear power for commercial ships has proved unsuccessful in other countries, the Russians have used nuclear propulsion for their giant ice-breakers. The first of these huge vessels was the Lenin. Commissioned in 1959 the ship, which had three nuclear reactors as her power plant, remained in service for 30 years. Although extremely expensive to run, the Lenin's cost was justified as her massive power was needed to punch a way through the ice in order to keep open the northern sea route stretching from Novaya Semla to the Bering Sea.

BOTNICA MULTI-PURPOSE ICE-BREAKER

The Botnica, a combined ice-breaker, tug and supply vessel, is one of the most advanced vessels of her type. Built in Finland, she was delivered in 1998 to the Finnish Maritime Administration (FMA). Botnica is run on a diesel-electric plant. Six packages of twin Caterpillar 3512B units connected to six ABB generators power a thruster system of two 5MW Azipods. The thrusters can be used to make a propeller wave that pushes broken ice away from the hull, leaving a wider channel for commercial merchant vessels to follow.

MEGA FACT

Ground effect occurs when air pressure under a wing increases as the wing gets closer to the surface. That pressure keeps the wing from wanting to touch that surface. When a wing is in 'ground effect,' it is basically riding on a cushion of air.

GLOSSARY

BOAT A small, open craft without any deck.

BOW The narrow front end of a ship, pointed to cut cleanly into the water.

DRAG The force created by the action of water against the hull and propeller of a ship that slows it down. Ships with long, narrow hulls and pointed ends usually suffer less drag than those with wide hulls and blunt ends.

MEGA FACT
Japan is the world's leading shipbuilding country.

HORSEPOWER (HP) A measurement of a ship's engine power, equivalent to 746 watts.

DRIVESHAFT The shaft that transmits power from the engine to the propeller in a ship. Also called the propeller shaft.

HYDRODYNAMICS The effects and forces produced by and on water when objects are moving through it.

KNOT One nautical mile per hour, or 1.85km.

PROPELLER A shaft, formed in the shape of a spiral, turned by the engine to drive a ship.

RADAR An instrument that uses radio waves to measure the distance to an object and its speed and direction.

RUDDER A flat plate hinged to the stern of a ship and used to steer the ship.

SHIP Generally, an ocean-going vessel with a deck.

SONAR A device that detects the location and what an object is underwater by using sound waves.

STABILISERS Fins projecting from the sides of the hull to help keep a ship steady.

SUPERCONDUCTING Having no electrical resistance. In metals, this occurs when they are cooled to very low temperatures.

THRUST The force that drives ships forward, provided by the turning action of the propellers, which throw a powerful surge of water backward.

THRUSTERS Extra propellers in the hull of a ship for moving sideways.

TURBINE ENGINE High-speed engines that work like the jets that power planes.

MEGA FACT

Today, a cargo ship is capable of producing the same amount of exhaust fumes as 10,000 cars!

INDEX

Publications:

✗ 100 Historic Ships in Full Color (US Edition) ISBN 0486420671
✗ All About Ships ISBN 1842150154
✗ All about Ships: Amazing Maritime Facts (US Edition) ISBN 1842150154
✗ Compendium of the World's Passenger Ships ISBN 0952358131
✗ Liners,Tankers, Merchant Ships 300 of the World's Greatest Commercial Vessels ISBN 1840134771
✗ Ships and Submarines (US Edition) ISBN 0613349458

Picture Credits

T=top; B=bottom; C=centre L=left R=right

Cover Beken of Cowes

3 T Kvaerner Masa-Yards, TC Beken of Cowes, C Irish ferries, BC Stephanie Maze/Corbis, B HDW Shipyard, Germany; 4-5 Kvaerner Masa-Yards, 5 T Man B&W; 6-7 Beken of Cowes; 7 T Mary Evan picture library; 8 T Hulton/Archive, B Mary Evans; 9 T Bettmann/Corbis, B Carl & Ann Purcell/Corbis; 10 T Beken of Cowes, 10B Beken of Cowes; 11 Hulton/Archives, 11T Hulton/Archives; 12 T Beken of Cowes, B Mary Evans Picture Library; 13 TIntertanko, B Kvaerner Masa-Yards; 14-15 B Irish Ferries, 15 T Paul Almasy/Corbis; 16 T Irish ferries, B Beken of Cowes, 17T Neil Rabinowitz/Corbis, 18 T P&O, B Austal; 19 T Carl & Ann Purcell/Corbis, B Sea Containers Services Ltd; 20-21 Stephanie Maze/Corbis; 21 T Hulton-Deutsch/Corbis; 22 T Peter Johnson/Corbis, B Hulton/Archives, 23 TL Shell Picture library, TR Joel W Rodger/Corbis, B Corbis; 24-25 HDW Shipyard, Germany; 25 Robert Harding/Digitalvision; 26-27 T HDW Shipyard, Germany, 26-27 B Kvaerner Masa-Yards; 28 T Science Photo Library, B Intertanko; 29 T Yevgeny Khaldei/Corbis, B AKER FinnYards; 30-31 Beken of Cowes.